GW01401269

Original title:
Too Cool for School, Literally

Author: Aurora Sinclair

ISBN HARDBACK: 978-9916-94-224-6
ISBN PAPERBACK: 978-9916-94-225-3

The Winter of our Minds

Snowflakes swirl, my thoughts drift wide,
Sipping cocoa, with nowhere to hide.
Math class waits, but I'd rather play,
In this frosty world where I laze all day.

Papers fly like winter flurries,
Homework's lost, oh, the worries!
But here in dreams, I take a stand,
Building castles in the sand.

Classroom Chronicles in a Snow Globe

Inside this globe, the desk is a sea,
Floating doodles, just you and me.
A teacher's voice like a Christmas bell,
While we giggle in our tiny shell.

Snowmen dance with a pencil's grace,
As equations swirl in this magical space.
The chalkboard's full, but so is my mind,
Lost in laughter, I'm blissfully blind.

Bits of Ice, Bursts of Insight

Ice cubes rattle in my cup,
As I try to keep my focus up.
Thoughts like icicles, sharp and bright,
But my attention takes a flight.

A sudden snowball rolls on by,
My ideas slip and surely fly.
With each splash, a laugh erupts,
In this winter wonderland, I'm happily stumped.

Snowy Banks of Creativity

Piled high like snow, my dreams take shape,
Each one a colorful, crazy escape.
Paper angels dance on the floor,
Every scribble opens a door.

My brain's a sled, racing downhill,
With giggles echoing—what a thrill!
In this classroom of icy delight,
I'll paint my world, bold and bright.

Chasing Winter's Wisdom

Snowflakes dance like glitter bright,
Frosted books reflecting light.
Teachers wear their woolly hats,
Learning's fun on chilly mats.

Homework's in a snowman's lap,
Lessons turned into a nap.
Sledding down the icy hill,
Who needs school when you've got thrill?

Chasing wisdom on the slopes,
Giggles burst like bubbles, hopes.
Winter's magic fills the air,
Smartness found in frosty flair.

The Dreamcatcher in a Snowstorm

Dreams get caught like flurries fly,
In swirling winds, oh me, oh my!
Reality takes a snowy break,
When snowmen learn to shake and bake.

Pencil's frozen, but who needs ink?
Writing's fun with snowdrift stink.
Falling dreams like frozen drops,
In this storm, the laughter hops.

Caught beneath the cozy eaves,
Where learning's just a game of leaves.
Let's make hot cocoa, not a test,
Chasing dreams where snowflakes rest.

Breath of Frost

Frosty breath on morning air,
Giggles hidden, unaware.
In icy halls, we slide and glide,
Life's a joke that we can ride.

Hot chocolate spills in empty rooms,
While teachers plot with paper brooms.
Crayons melt in sun's warm rays,
Who knew winter could be such a phase?

With frosted brains and chilly toes,
Laughter's wind where no one knows.
Absurdities wrapped in chill,
Let's skip class and dance at will.

Whisper of Books

Books are whispered tales untold,
In jumbled pages, laughter's bold.
A chapter filled with snowball fights,
Echoes of joy in quiet nights.

My pencil doodles on the side,
While teachers sigh and take the ride.
Let's build knowledge like a fort,
In classrooms turned to winter sport.

Reading under blankets thick,
Where stories fly and words can flick.
With every laugh, we learn the tricks,
Of frosty days and frozen kicks.

Icy Reflections in a Warm World

Mirrors show us frosty cheer,
In a world that feels so sheer.
Goofing off in icy dreams,
Life's a snowball — bursting seams!

Laughter echoes off the walls,
Where snowflakes dance and knowledge calls.
Each class is painted white with fun,
In this chill, we've just begun.

Sipping cocoa, giggling loud,
Warming up beneath the cloud.
In this space, we find our place,
Icy reflections, a warm embrace.

The Floating Iceberg of Understanding

In the classroom, I sit with a grin,
While thoughts of my bed begin to spin.
My mind's like an iceberg, afloat in the sea,
Drifting on dreams, not learning from me.

The teacher's voice echoes, but my ears won't comply,
Why learn about math when I could just fly?
With snacks for my brain and a pillow for thought,
In a world of distractions, knowledge's been caught.

Subzero Study Sessions

Piles of textbooks, they chill on my desk,
Like frozen yogurt, it's just a big mess.
I opened one up, but my brain went on strike,
Thoughts turned to snowflakes, drifting alike.

With hot cocoa dreams and homework a haze,
I laugh at my notes like they're stuck in a maze.
The clock ticks in freeze-frame, time stops in mid-air,
Subzero in focus, I'm going nowhere.

Lessons Drifting on Ice

Floating on ice, my attention drifts past,
Like a penguin on skirts, too clumsy to last.
I scribble in circles, but it's all just for fun,
Learning's a game, and I'm not on the run.

A snowball of wisdom, it just won't take shape,
While I frolic in thoughts, dreaming of cape.
With laughter and antics, I float through each hour,
In a land filled with dreams, I'm the school's finest
flower.

Cold-Weather Contemplations

In winter's embrace, I ponder my fate,
Choosing blankets and snacks over homework's debate.
The textbooks grow chilly, forgotten in place,
While visions of snowballs dance on my face.

The wind howls outside, a wild winter tune,
Each page of my study feels like a cartoon.
With my mind on the slopes, I glide through the day,
Let's face it, this school thing's just too far away!

College of Coldness

In halls of frost, where laughter sings,
Students dodge the chill that winter brings.
With hats askew and boots that slide,
Knowledge frosted, but spirits wide.

Classes taught by icicle professors,
Who chill the room with frosty gestures.
Hot cocoa fuels the brainy chat,
While snowmen guard the welcome mat.

Snowflakes and Scholars

Snowflakes twirl like thoughts in flight,
As scholars debate in the pale moonlight.
Books are stacking, but so is the snow,
Learning is lighter, where few dare to go.

With shovels sharp as sharpened pens,
They dig through theories where winter ends.
Coffee spills like new found lore,
On icy desks, we want to explore!

Learning with a Chill

Chill in the air and jokes in the air,
We study math while freezing in pairs.
Notes get messy with flakes from above,
Laughter defrosts what we're dreaming of.

Profs with frost beards, spinning yarns,
While papers fall like snow to the lawns.
With witty banter, we keep it light,
In winter's grasp, we shine bright!

The Icy Embrace of Curiosity

Curiosity wrapped in a blanket of freeze,
As questions drift like snow on the breeze.
We ponder deep in the chilly air,
While laughter echoes, without a care.

Knowledge drips like melting ice,
Each answer found feels like a slice.
Exploring worlds with a frosty grin,
In this embrace, let the fun begin!

Academic Disdain in Denim

In jeans so faded, I stroll with flair,
Teachers frown, they don't quite care.
Books piled high, yet I just sigh,
Who needs grades? I'm too fly!

The clock keeps ticking, I'm lost in dream,
Math equations? Nah, I'll just scheme.
History's boring, like watching paint,
But my sneakers? Oh, they really ain't.

Frosty Thoughts in Classrooms

In class I sit, my mind's a drift,
While winter winds bring nature's gift.
Snowflakes dance outside my view,
While I imagine a chilly brew.

Teachers drone on, but I'm not fazed,
Counting the minutes, I'm quite amazed.
Days blur by in frosty haze,
Yet my cool vibe? It always stays.

The Homework Heist

Under the desk, my phone glows bright,
Texting my pals to plan tonight.
Homework is due, but who can care?
Stealing time like it's a dare.

I weigh the odds, a scheme so slick,
"Just one more episode, then I'll kick—"
The stress of tasks, a playful game,
Yet somehow I'm still earning fame.

Cramming Under Cover

Midnight strikes, the clock's my foe,
Papers scattered, all in a row.
Cramming hard, with snacks in hand,
A last-minute plan, my own bandstand.

I blink awake, the cats just yawn,
Books in disarray, a thought's upon.
But all this chaos, oh what a ride,
Learning's best with pizza by my side!

Glacial Currents of Thought

In the hallways of frozen dreams,
Knowledge drips like melting creams.
Students breeze with frosty flair,
Laughter echoes, chilled in air.

Homework's like a snowball fight,
Dodging facts, oh what a sight!
Frosty fingers type away,
Dreams of warmth in sunlit sway.

Chilled Ambition

I throw my cap in icy glee,
Plans as lofty as a snow-capped tree.
Chilling at the top, no stress,
Learning's fun, I must confess.

Slides of knowledge, gliding fast,
With witty quips, this spell is cast.
In this cool ride, I never fear,
While sipping ice-cold lemonade here.

The Ice Queen of Academia

Crowned in snowflakes, bold and bright,
I reign o'er tests without a fright.
With frosty wit, I craft my schemes,
Lessons dance like winter dreams.

No one dares to cross my path,
Laughter flies like a snowy math.
In classrooms cold, I'm warm with cheer,
For rule of fun, I'm the pioneer!

Snowstorm of Ideas

Thoughts whip round like winter winds,
In this blizzard, joy begins.
Ideas flurry, tumble, race,
A frosty smile upon my face.

I build snowmen of knowledge bright,
Crafting dreams in pure delight.
With every flake a brand-new fun,
The snowstorm rages, yet we're one!

On the Edge of the Ice

Skating past the teacher's glare,
I glide like I just don't care.
Notes of math float on by,
While I dream of the big blue sky.

Lunchroom battles, pizza slices,
Dodgeball fights with all the vices.
We laugh and slip on frozen floors,
Who knew school had so many scores?

Homework? Nope, I'm busy now,
Learning moves, oh yes, I vow.
Pencils drop, oh what a scene,
It's an ice rink, not a routine!

Racing sleds and laughing loud,
Books on ice, we draw a crowd.
Classes can wait, we're off the hook,
The only test is our next flip book.

Glacial Thoughts in the Hallway

Wandering slow like a frozen stream,
Hallways feel like a daydream.
Calculators? Right, they don't apply,
When your brain is frozen like a pie.

Teachers talk, but I just zone,
Drawing snowmen on my phone.
Wisdom drips like melting ice,
I'd rather roll some dice.

A frozen lunch, it's gourmet,
Mystery meat in a frozen display.
I'll trade a sandwich for a laugh,
And scatter crumbs for a crazy staff.

Swooshing by with style and grace,
Nothing beats this frozen place.
Thoughts like snowflakes whirl and sway,
In a winter wonderland of play.

Arctic Breezes and Wise Faces

Frigid air and frosty cheer,
We've got nothing to truly fear.
Chilly fingers write our fate,
Cracking jokes about the date.

Pop quizzes chilling at the door,
No one's here, just ice galore.
I sip my cocoa, soft and sweet,
While the smart kids admit defeat.

Breezes blow through the cracks and doors,
But laughter echoes, and it soars.
Nothing's cooler than this game,
We'll all win, who needs the fame?

Chilling on seats, skating in line,
We perfected our frosty design.
Math is melting, plans do freeze,
We're the masters of cooling breeze.

Lessons on Ice

Today's lesson? Don't slip and fall,
Safety first, but we're having a ball.
Geometry shapes on icy ground,
It's the coolest math we've found.

Teachers say that grades are key,
But not when you ski with me!
Rolling laughter, sliding sounds,
In these freezes, joy abounds.

Writing essays? Oh what a tease,
When all I want is skating with ease.
Homework melts like the morning dew,
I'll ace the test on what we do!

Late submissions, a frosty tale,
Turning in snowflakes, we won't fail.
We're learning life, on this slick stage,
In this class, we write our own page.

The Cool Connoisseur of Class

Chillin' in the front, got my shades on tight,
Teacher's droning on, but I'm feeling just right.
Papers flying high like a well-cast net,
Making friends with snacks, my best mindset.

Homework? Nah, I just doodle and smile,
Structuring my thoughts in a leisurely style.
My desk is a throne, I reign supreme,
Classroom comedy's my ultimate dream.

Got the jokes and quips, I'm the class clown,
When the bell rings loud, I'll be outta town.
Lunchroom giggles echo down the hall,
Who knew being cool could risk it all?

Signed up for the course of shenanigans bright,
Capturing moments, everything feels right.
With my crown of laughter, I take my stand,
In the school of life, I'm the cool brand.

Glacial Lulls of Engagement

Snoozin' in class, it's a frosty affair,
The clock's tickin' slow, I hardly care.
When the teacher calls, I freeze in my seat,
But daydreaming adventures can't be beat.

Notes start to float, like a snowflake's grace,
Words turn to ice in this dull, frozen place.
I scribble my thoughts, abstract art on the page,
In this wintery trance, I'm a wise old sage.

Chillin' on facts while my mind does a spin,
Classes like glaciers, where do I begin?
Yet laughter erupts like a snowball fight,
Warming up moments, igniting delight.

Lunch is my break, a thawing of fun,
Where the best tales are told, battles won.
Recess reigns king, our laughter will soar,
In this winter wonderland, who could ask for more?

Frosted Futures Await

Classroom adventures await like a chill,
Learning's a mountain, but I've got the will.
With ice cream dreams and a sprinkle of flair,
I coast through the lessons, without a care.

Future's a canvas, painted in frost,
One laugh at a time, we never feel lost.
The carefree moments stick, like snow on the ground,
Each giggle echoes, a sweet, joyful sound.

Got a map to tomorrow, let's skate on the path,
Finding joy in the journey's the best kind of math.
With buddies beside me, it's a frosty pursuit,
We'll conquer the world, and we'll look so cute.

Slips and tumbles may lead to new sights,
With snowflakes of laughter, we shine oh so bright.
In classrooms of ice, we'll dance and we'll play,
Frosted futures await, come what may!

The Snowman's Lesson Plan

A snowman stood with a chalk in hand,
Teaching lessons in a winter land.
His pupils were penguins, eager and bright,
Learning how to slide through the frosty night.

With a carrot nose and a scarf so red,
He taught them math as they balanced their heads.
Subtraction with snowballs, addition with ice,
Calculating angles was rather nice!

But when it came to sports, oh what a thrill,
Snowball dodgeball gave them quite the chill.
With each icy throw, they'd giggle and cheer,
The snowman chuckled, "Now that's a career!"

By the end of the day, they'd danced in delight,
A snowman's lesson plan, truly a sight.
With laughter and fun, they all agreed,
Coolness is better when learning is freed!

Polar Vortex of Knowledge

In the polar vortex, the wisdom flows,
Chilling ideas that nobody knows.
The walrus is grading with blubbery flair,
While seals take the tests in the frosty air.

Snowflakes fall gently on notes that they take,
Teaching the science of a snowball's make.
The wise old owl tells stories of yore,
As the students listen, they beg for more.

Together they brainstorm, ideas collide,
Building ice castles, oh what a ride!
The bells ring clear, "It's time to go!"
But knowledge stays frozen in the hearts, you know.

Off they slide down the ice in glee,
Learning in winter, so wild and free.
In polar vortex, adventures ignite,
Where laughter and learning take glorious flight!

Frostbite Wisdom

Frostbite wisdom, a chilly delight,
As snowflakes whisper secrets at night.
A wise old fox with a twinkle in eye,
Shares tales of school under blankets awry.

With snowball fights tucked into study breaks,
They learn the truth through the shivering shakes.
Each lesson's a laugh, wrapped in a conjure,
Like counting the stars through a starlit wander.

The chipmunks chatter, with knowledge they boast,
In the heart of winter, they learn the most.
Navigating snowdrifts, they conquer the cold,
Finding treasures in piles of white and bold.

So grab your mittens, let's make a dash,
For frostbite wisdom, a playful splash.
In this winter wonder, let giggles ensue,
Learning's an adventure, funny and true!

Learning Under a Frosted Sky

Under a frosted sky, the laughter's high,
Snowflakes twirl like notes as they fly.
The classroom's a sled, who's ready to race?
With frosty textbooks, they make quite the face.

The teacher, a bear in a cozy old coat,
Gives lessons on icebergs that float and gloat.
Math on the whiteboard with chalk made of snow,
Counting the sleds that go to and fro.

With every slide down the shimmering hills,
Learning's a rush; it sends joyful chills.
Art projects sparkle, glittering frost,
Creating a masterpiece that can't be lost.

As day turns to night, and the stars all twinkle,
They shout, "More learning!" as they all tinkle.
Under a frosted sky, with hearts aglow,
In the magic of winter, there's so much to know!

The Freeze Frame of Education

When teachers start to lecture, we drift, we float,
Dreaming of snowballs and hot cocoa coats.
Homework lies in piles, like frost on the grass,
As we plan our escape, it's a real blast!

The bell rings loud, but we're still in a daze,
Building snowmen in our brains, lost in a maze.
The grades may feel chilly, but we wear a grin,
As we scheme for the weekend, let the fun begin!

Pencils are icicles, pens frozen and stuck,
Our notes are so cool, they'll need a warm-up.
With textbooks as sleds, we slide through our days,
Laughing while learning in the snow's chilly haze.

So here's to the laughter, the pranks we will pull,
Each class is a blizzard, with wind so full.
We skate through the lessons, with style and flair,
In this frozen kingdom, we hardly repair.

A Winter's Chill in Study Rooms

In corners we giggle, it's all so absurd,
Books lined up like snowflakes, each page a bird.
We burst into laughter, like snowmen in rows,
While the teacher rolls eyes, and hopelessly goes.

Pop quizzes await, like ice on the ground,
But we're armoring up with a smile all around.
Time ticks like icicles, hanging by threads,
As we plot our escape while dodging our beds.

Draw graphs made of snow, with rulers of ice,
We doodle our plans, oh isn't this nice?
A snowball's our weapon, in class it's a game,
Instead of our homework, we're just here for fame.

So come join the fun! Let's chill in our spree,
Forget all the textbooks, come play with me!
We'll mix laughs with lessons, till the final bell rings,
In this winter of wonder, let laughter take wings.

Frigid Futures

Chilling in class, we plot our escape,
Dreaming of summers where we can reshape.
A brain freeze of knowledge, it's cool but it's tough,
Yet laughter is warmer; we're never enough.

With each icy glance from the teacher's brave eyes,
We scribble our notes and concoct silly lies.
Group projects turn frosty, with squabbles so spry,
Yet we giggle through numbers, our laughter's the high.

So many directions, like snowdrifts we brace,
We walk through the halls with a smile on our face.
When math gets too hard, we just think of dessert,
Our fridge is the limit, let's wear our new shirt!

The future seems frozen, yet we dance in the cold,
Making snow angels, being brave and bold.
So here's to the scholars of frosty delight,
In this school full of fun, we're the kids that ignite.

The Cool Kid's Guide to Class

Step one, strut in like a snowstorm on cue,
With a wink, and a grin, make the day brand new.
Throw in some jokes, let the laughter not cease,
Class is an ice rink, so let's glide with ease.

Homework's a mountain, but we'll ski right on through,
Just pack up the fun like it's hot cocoa brew.
Group chats a flurry, with sarcasm to spare,
Trading inside jokes like we just don't care.

Throw paper snowballs, hit the ceiling with flair,
Class will freeze over while we giggle and stare.
Grades might be chilly, but our spirits stay warm,
With a chill in the air that'll keep us from harm.

So grab all your friends, time to rewrite the rules,
With laughter and mischief, we'll shatter the tools.
The cool kids are here; let's create quite a scene,
In this winter of study, we'll rule like a queen!

The Polar Path to Discovery

In a land where snowflakes dance with glee,
Learning's an adventure, wild and free.
Textbooks chillin' in an icy breeze,
While students giggle and do as they please.

Math problems float like snowmen in the air,
With each wrong answer, laughter we share.
Science experiments turn to icy blasts,
And history's tales become hilarious casts.

Ice-Capped Creativity

Creativity frosts like a winter delight,
With crayons melting under the moonlight.
Art classes feel like a frosty retreat,
Where paint turns to globs that slide off your seat.

Crafting snowflakes from paper and glue,
Each masterpiece garners a chuckle or two.
We sculpt with laughter, and giggles ensue,
An ice-capped creativity that sparkles anew.

Frosted Feats of Learning

In the class where winter's spirit shines,
Geography involves mapping frosty pines.
Literature's tales are best read with a grin,
Every plot twist covered in snow from within.

History's giants slip on their own turf,
While plotting a course through their frozen surf.
Every detour leads to humor galore,
As we munch on hot cocoa, begging for more.

Beyond the Ice Wall of Examination

Exams here are more like glacier games,
Sliding through questions, avoiding the flames.
Teachers throw quizzes like snowballs in jest,
While we plot our escape with great zest.

Studying's a snowball fight under the sun,
Where answers are scattered, and puns are the fun.
Beyond the icy wall, we find a warm glow,
In laughter and learning, just let it flow.

Chill Vibes on Campus

Sunglasses on, we're feeling great,
Skipping class, it's our fate.
Sidewalks glisten in the sun,
Life's a game, we just won.

Backpacks packed with snacks and cheer,
Who needs books? We're pioneers.
Grabbing smoothies, feeling free,
School's just not the place to be.

Laughing loudly, making friends,
In our world, the fun never ends.
While others study, we explore,
Our coolness opens every door.

The Art of Not Appearing

We master the art of the ghost,
Invisible, we like it most.
Professors call, but we just fade,
A ninja trick, we're so well-made.

Hallway meetings, a stealthy glance,
Dodging lectures like a dance.
In the cafeteria, we blend right in,
Part-time magicians, where to begin?

No need for homework or to cram,
We'll ace this test—we still can!
With pizza slices, we plot and scheme,
A perfect life, or so we dream.

Ice in the Hallways

Chilly vibes in every glance,
We strut and slide, the cool kids' dance.
Lockers creak, a silent laugh,
Our ice-cold presence in each hallway path.

Skating past in casual style,
No rush to learn, we take a while.
Frosty jokes and smiles abound,
In our own universe, we're school-renowned.

Every corner holds a secret smile,
Who needs class? We'll stay awhile.
The bell rings loud, but we won't go,
We've mastered the art of 'just say no.'

Edges of Nonchalance

Leaning back in that old classroom,
We're the shadows, never gloom.
With a smirk, we nod and sigh,
Too calm for books, we're flying high.

Pencil in hand, doodling away,
Laughing at rules that lead us astray.
Chillin' hard, we hold our ground,
With every chuckle, the fun is found.

Teachers frown, but we don't care,
Absurdity hangs thick in the air.
In this bubble, we float with ease,
Too laid-back to feel the freeze.

Hall Passes and Half Smiles

Hall passes flutter like paper airplanes,
Sneaking out with mischief in our veins.
Teachers shout, but we just grin,
Ready for fun that's about to begin.

Lockers creak like an old wooden door,
Contents spill out, who could ask for more?
Notes and snacks stacked in a heap,
We hide our laughter, but secrets we keep.

Skipped math for the thrill of a snack,
Throwing our cares in a playful attack.
Half smiles shared, we race down the hall,
Living our rule-breaking dream, we stand tall.

Ringing bells lead us to hide and seek,
Time's our friend, and joy's what we speak.
When the day ends, we dart for the gate,
Chasing the sunset, laughing at fate.

Doodles of Daydreams

Pencils scribble in a chaotic dance,
Lines on paper weave a curious chance.
Math formulas turn into silly birds,
While history fades in a wave of words.

The teacher's lecture fades into a blur,
As doodles come alive, a cheerful stir.
Monsters roar in the margins of notes,
While we plot our escape in wild little boats.

Colored pencils are heroes in disguise,
In a world of creativity, our laughter flies.
Cartoons leap from the edges, full of cheer,
While schoolwork waits, forgotten, in fear.

Ringing laughter fills the classroom air,
Each daydream crafted with playful flair.
When the bell tolls, we leap with delight,
Leaving behind reality, embracing the light.

Swagger in the Seats

Slouching back with a confident air,
We wear our swagger like a comfy chair.
Fingers drumming on tabletops like drums,
Bouncing to rhythms that laughter becomes.

Witty remarks fly like rubber bands,
While teachers lecture on boring demands.
We trade inside jokes, knowing the score,
School's just a stage, we're begging for more.

The classroom's our stage, the world's our script,
With mischief and giggles, we've tightly gripped.
While everyone studies, we plot our fun,
Crafting a moment, our day just begun.

When the clock ticks down, we dance out the door,
With swagger in each step, we crave even more.
A day's worth of humor, we can't help but claim,
In the grand school saga, we're leading the game.

When the Bell Rings for Freedom

The clock gives a jingle, a sweet chime call,
We bounce from our seats, it's time to enthrall.
A stampede of laughter fills every hall,
Escape is upon us, let's chance it all.

Backpacks slung low, with snacks to devour,
We dash outside, claiming the hour.
Fields stretch like dreams under the sun,
Chasing adventure 'til day's finally done.

Whispers of plans bounce like balls on the green,
Picnic blankets spread, where chill meets the scene.
No homework in sight, just smiles to share,
Moments of friendship float thick in the air.

When the day fades, and the sun sinks low,
We sneak in more giggles, casting our glow.
Each bell rings a promise of laughter and cheer,
In the freedom of play, we hold what is dear.

The Cool Factor of Cutting Class

Skipping classes feels so nice,
Freedom calls, I roll the dice.
With friends we laugh, we run and hide,
In the sun, we take our ride.

Textbooks weigh a ton, what a bore!
Who needs those when there's so much more?
Ice cream cones and sunny parks,
Life outside has all the sparks.

A teacher's call, 'No more delay!'
But here we are, we're on our way.
Run away from the schoolyard gate,
Finding joy, it's never late.

Lunch in hand, we strut around,
In our world, we feel so sound.
Skiving off, just living free,
Now that's the ultimate decree!

Casual Fridays on a Wednesday

Wearing PJs, oh what a sight,
Why save it for Friday night?
Jumping in, it's midweek cheer,
Fashion rules, we steer clear.

Socks with sandals? Yes, indeed!
Who says a wardrobe shouldn't lead?
With every step, we break that mold,
Style so bold, it never gets old.

Teachers gasp as we pass by,
"What are they wearing?" Oh my, oh my!
But who could care? We dance and prance,
Unified in our wacky stance.

A lunchroom throne, we sit in glee,
Tray of snacks, it's you and me.
Casual vibes, our only quest,
Wednesday brings out our very best!

Cool Shadows in Lecture Halls

In a lecture hall, shadows play,
While the teacher drones away.
Whispers and giggles, a mischievous crew,
Plotting the next big thing to do.

Beneath the desk, a game of cards,
Teaching math? We'd rather mix yards.
Doodles in books, sketching away,
Our secret language, the art of delay.

Falling asleep? Don't be absurd,
In our dreams, it's no longer blurred.
Chasing unicorns, ruling the skies,
Conquering worlds with our sleepy eyes.

When the bell rings, we jump in cheer,
Learning's fine, but no need to steer.
Off we go to the light outside,
In our shadows, we take pride!

The Unread Textbook

On my desk, it sits in dust,
Promises of knowledge, not a must.
Flipping pages? What a bore!
Let's just Netflix, who needs more?

Cramming in before exams,
Wishing instead for social jams.
Textbook tales of wars and math,
But I'd rather laugh than do the path.

Future dreams? A mystery still,
With potential, we just chill.
"Hey, did you read?" a friend will ask,
I chuckle softly, it's quite the task.

Life is short, fun's on the line,
So I'll keep dancing, feeling fine.
That textbook waits, I'll set it free,
Priorities set, it's you and me!

Breezy Breaks Between Lectures

The bell rings loud, it's time to flee,
With snacks in hand, we roam carefree.
Outside the halls, we tell tall tales,
Swapping laughs like pirate jails.

A stroll beneath the sun so bright,
Chasing dreams, oh what a sight!
Classroom woes just fade away,
We live for this absurd with play.

The ladybug on my shoulder beams,
She knows the secret of our dreams.
With whispers sweet, we plot our schemes,
A world outside the textbook themes.

As laughter echoes, time does fly,
Who needs the stress, just you and I?
We juggle woes like clumsy fools,
In breezy breaks, we break the rules.

The Unruly Rebel's Guide

Grab your snacks, the clock ticks slow,
Skip the rules, we steal the show!
A wink, a nod, let's cause a fuss,
Who needs lectures? Come ride the bus.

Forgotten notes that gather dust,
In the land of 'Why not?' we trust.
Rules are made for breaking, friend,
We'll start the trends, not just pretend.

With swagger bold and hats askew,
Defying norms, we'll paint it blue.
Chapters missed; we're still the best,
In this outcast life, we find our zest.

So gather round, all ye who dare,
In mischief's light, beyond compare.
Raise your voice, let's sing the tune,
To rebel hearts, beneath the moon.

Coolness in Professorial Eyes

The professor scowls, but wait, just look,
With glasses perched, the coolest book.
Their lecture drags, but here we sit,
Pretending we care while sharing wit.

A smirk escapes, they catch the joke,
Secret giggles like sweet smoke.
They lecture on, oblivious sway,
While we dream of a beachy day.

Coolness thrives in awkward grace,
In their stern eyes, a hint, a trace.
Quite the puzzle, a quirky riddle,
Professors grooving, though not a little.

In discord's rhythm, we intertwine,
This school of chaos, so divine.
Let's raise a toast to these moments rare,
Coolness reigns without a care.

Latitude of Indifference

In the hallway's stretch, we saunter slow,
With lazy grins, we steal the show.
Assignments loom like stormy skies,
Yet we bask in our sweet alibis.

The coffee brews, the laughter flows,
Ignorance, our crown for those.
We twirl and dance in carefree swing,
While textbooks frown, we laugh and cling.

With every chat, we push the bounds,
In this realm, laughter resounds.
While others worry, we take our time,
Dining on humor, sweet as a rhyme.

In this latitude where rules dissolve,
Our sunny spirits completely evolve.
So let them lecture, let them strive,
In this blissful void, we come alive.

The Frosty Pursuit of Knowledge

In a classroom made of ice,
Laughter echoes, oh so nice.
Snowflakes dance upon each word,
Knowledge flies, like it's absurd.

Chalk sticks are frozen, what a sight,
Pencils shiver, but spirits are bright.
Teachers wear mittens, learn with glee,
Who knew math could be so free?

Homework glows like frosty stars,
Backpacks filled with candy bars.
Geometry's fun when snowflakes fall,
Let's build a fort, and skip the call!

At recess, we ski on the floor,
Science experiments? More like a chore!
But in this icy land, we find cheer,
Education's chill, let's give a cheer!

Cold Truths in Warm Hearts

With a smile that's bright as the sun,
Hot chocolate's ready, oh what fun!
Textbooks bundled in winter gear,
Who knew knowledge could be so dear?

Chalkboards shimmer with frostbite ink,
Students giggle, pause to think.
Lessons warm, like cocoa's embrace,
A curious mind finds its place.

On icy chairs, we discuss the trends,
Wearing scarves, we make new friends.
History taught with a snowball fight,
Learning here feels just right.

Classrooms filled with jokes and cheer,
Forget the stress, we've nothing to fear.
With hearts so warm, it's perfectly clear,
In this shivery place, fun's always near!

Brain Freeze Bookshelves

Books lined up in frosty rows,
Page by page, the excitement grows.
Reading under blankets, snug and tight,
Who knew stories could take flight?

Library aisles filled with snowy tales,
Imaginations riding winter gales.
Every chapter brings a laugh,
Makes us forget we had to draft.

Spines are chilled, but laughter's warm,
Characters' antics break the norm.
Dressed like penguins, we roam around,
In this cool space, fun is found.

And when the bell rings, we cheer and shout,
Books keep us guessing, without a doubt.
In this winter wonderland of thought,
Who knew learning could be so sought?

A Winter Class of Wonders

Snowflakes twirl around our heads,
While we're taught to think and spread.
Math equations, taken too lightly,
Turn into art, oh so sprightly!

Science lessons freeze in the air,
Accidental snowballs hide the glare.
History's tales wrapped in ice,
Learning with giggles, oh so nice.

Art class has crayons in chilly hues,
Painting dreams of warm summer views.
Creativity blooms when the cold winds blow,
In this frosty class, our imaginations flow.

So come along, don't miss the fun,
In our winter room, there's room for everyone.
With smiles and laughter, every hour,
In this class, we bloom like flowers!

Frigid Fame in Learning Spaces

Chilly winds in class today,
The teacher's lost her way.
Ice cream cones for lunch, my friend,
We'll laugh and chill until the end.

Textbooks stacked like frozen piles,
We trade them in for snowball smiles.
The bell rings loud, we run and glide,
Skipping lessons, taking pride.

Homework begins to freeze in place,
While we paint the teacher's face.
Gloves on hands and books in thaw,
Our icy feats, they leave them in awe.

In this frosty frolic, we'll survive,
Who needs grades when we can thrive?
With laughter echoing through the halls,
We rule the school with snowball brawls.

Exploration in Icy Realms

Adventures on the snowy hill,
Math quizzes? Oh, what a thrill!
Sliding down with frosty cheer,
Avoiding math, it's perfectly clear.

Wandering through the frozen pines,
Shivering, we share our signs.
Chasing snowflakes, counting fun,
While inside, the learning's done.

A snowman dressed in someone's coat,
Stands tall where we used to gloat.
We build our fun, it's quite absurd,
In icy realms, we've got the word.

Escaping books, reject the throne,
We claim the slopes, we're not alone.
In winter's grip, we find our way,
Where laughter leads, there we shall play.

The Frosty Light of Intelligence

Brains freeze in this wintry plight,
But laughter shines, all sparkly bright.
We skip the tests with knowing grins,
In the frosty glow, our fun begins.

Shovels out, let's clear the path,
Navigating through a snowy math.
Piled high with dreams, our minds aglow,
Playing instead, we steal the show.

Diagramming snowflakes in the air,
Calculating joy, without a care.
Who needs equations, facts, or rules?
We're the royalty of ice-cold schools.

A classroom wrapped in winter's charm,
Where frosty laughter keeps us warm.
With every snowball, wisdom flies,
In this frosty light, we reach the skies.

Snowy Hideaways of Thought

In caverns made of frozen dreams,
We plot and scheme with silly themes.
Hideaway from lessons there,
Where thoughts drift softly through the air.

Snowdrifts piled like unturned pages,
In winter's class, we're funny sages.
Creating worlds with icy flair,
Constructive chaos everywhere.

We build our forts with sticks and twine,
Write secret notes in the frost's design.
Math homework? Never see it through,
While snowflakes dance in the chilly blue.

Our laughter fills the crystal skies,
In snowy nooks, we'll claim the prize.
So let them ask, "What's the score?"
In this frosty hideaway, we'll learn once more.

Articulate Adventures in Learning

In a classroom of snow, minds dance with glee,
Knowledge on ice, like it's wild and free.
With pencils like icicles, we scribble and play,
Teachers in mittens, teaching all day.

Laughter erupts as we frost the facts,
Words slide like sleds on well-planned tracks.
Concepts like snowflakes that twirl and glide,
In this blizzard of wisdom, we take it in stride.

Textbooks like snowmen with hats quite absurd,
Facts packed like snowballs, oh haven't you heard?
Each quiz takes a plunge, like diving in frost,
In the winter of learning, we never feel lost.

So bring on the lessons, let's cheer and explore,
Adventure awaits through the classroom door.
With laughter and learning, we zoom through the freeze,
In this frosty kingdom, we learn with great ease.

The Frosty Frontier of Education

On a frontier of ice, where we gather each day,
Lessons float gently on winter's ballet.
We carve out our knowledge with laughter and cheer,
In this chilly retreat, our minds have no fear.

With every cool project, our spirits ignite,
Like fireworks in snow, making learning feel bright.
Classrooms like igloos, cozy and warm,
In this frosty adventure, we weather the storm.

From math to intrigue, we surf on the breeze,
Mixing equations like warm cups of freeze.
Exploring the world with a grin on our face,
In this winter wonder, we sprint with our pace.

So hats off to learning, let's slide into fun,
In this frosty domain, we're all number one.
Through snowdrifts of knowledge, we'll skillfully roam,
On this frosty frontier, we've made our own home.

Cool Kids and Comet Dreams

Under the glow of a frosty moonlight,
We dream of comets soaring out of sight.
With snowy hairdos and spirit so bold,
Our laughter erupts like tales to be told.

Math equations dance like stars in the sky,
Making neat constellations as we try to fly.
In our starry-eyed missions, we venture and zoom,
Through galaxies of knowledge, we burst forth with
whom.

Lunch boxes packed with the finest of treats,
Sandwiches dressed like astronauts on sweets.
In our cosmic playground, we race and we spin,
With gravity-defying laughter, let the learning begin!

Cool kids unite with our comet-bound schemes,
Creating our future, fueled by our dreams.
In this galaxy of fun, watch us all gleam,
With each joyful lesson, we're living the dream.

Winter Wits and Clever Chills

In winter's embrace, our wits come alive,
With clever chills flying, we bounce and we jive.
We crack up the codes like codes in a game,
Navigating knowledge, we're never the same.

Science experiments like fizzles in frost,
Making bubbles of laughter, it's never a loss.
With snowflakes as notes, we compose our grand score,
In a symphony of giggles, we always want more.

We roam through the books like explorers at play,
Digging for treasures in every old page.
Erasing our worries with jokes on the side,
In this winter wonderland, we take in our stride.

So let's bundle up in our thoughts and ideas,
With warmth in our hearts and not one trace of fears.
In this chilly uprising, where laughter spills thrills,
We're the champions of winter, with our winter wits and
chills.

An Icy Spark in the Mind

I woke up late with frosty hair,
Dreams of class just float in air.
Pajamas on, I grab a snack,
In my mind, no study track.

The math books sit, they're gathering dust,
A snowman's built, it's a must.
With hot cocoa, I sip and sigh,
Who needs math when snowflakes fly?

In every corner, laughter grows,
While homework sleeps in winter's prose.
The only test that's on my mind,
Is how to sled and what to find.

So here I sit, with snack in hand,
Pondering dreams of snow and sand.
The school bell rings, let others fret,
For frozen minds are the best, you bet!

Brain Freeze Breakthroughs

On a frosty day, I took a sip,
Of icy slush that made me flip.
My head went numb, a chill so bright,
Ideas danced like snowflakes light.

The teacher called, but I just stared,
Thoughts of frozen lollies flared.
Brain freeze hits; I felt so smart,
Inventing ways to skip math art.

My buddies laughed at my bright ideas,
Like making snowmen instead of gears.
So we stumbled out of that dull room,
For fun, not facts, would make us bloom.

With brain freeze wisdom in our sight,
We learned that fun is pure delight.
Next time I study, I'll do it right—
With icy treats, oh, what a sight!

The Chill of Ignorance

In the land of snow, I chose to play,
While lessons drifted far away.
Textbooks closed, my heart was light,
Why worry about math tonight?

The chill of ignorance felt so fine,
While others studied, I sipped on wine.
My brain set sail on a frosty breeze,
Ignoring the homework with such ease.

I built a fort, it stood so proud,
While formulas fell, I cheered aloud.
A ruler's edge could hardly cut,
Through layers of snow where I was shut.

As laughter echoed around that hill,
The chill of ignorance gave me a thrill.
For with each snowball, I found my glee,
While others buried their brains, not me!

Winter's Wisdom Weaving

The snowflakes fall like little dreams,
While I avoid the teacher's screams.
Wrapped in blankets, I sip my drink,
Who needs to listen? I start to think.

In winter's grasp, the world is still,
No classrooms now, just snow to thrill.
With every flake, my mind spins round,
Creativity blooms where I'm tightly bound.

The icy slides and snowball fights,
Bring better lessons than the nights.
Each laugh is knowledge, every cheer,
In this frozen land, I have no fear.

So I embrace the chill within,
Where winter's wisdom is my kin.
In frosty fields, I find my way,
With fun as my guide, I choose to play!

Laughter in the Library

Whispers float between the shelves,
As giggles spill like quiet elves.
Books stacked high with secrets bold,
Yet laughter breaks the quiet mold.

A pencil rolls, a paper plane,
Tickling heads like a light rain.
Learning hides behind the jest,
In this nook, we find our fest.

Librarian's gaze like a hawk's stare,
While under tables, jokes we share.
The stories wait, the tales untold,
But laughter's worth its weight in gold.

In this haven where silence looms,
We sprinkle joy with silly tunes.
A secret giggle, a whispered tease,
In this wild world, we find our ease.

The Nonchalant Notebook

Pages turned with a casual swing,
In the back row, where chaos can cling.
Drawings dance across the sheets,
While wisdom takes a backseat.

Ink stains like my morning brew,
Mismatched scrawl, a creative view.
My notebook winks, it knows the score,
Learning lessons? Not a bore.

With doodles that could start a fight,
Maths and quotes blend wrong and right.
Once serious, now a show of flair,
A laugh erupts, I don't care.

Who says notes must stay in line?
My pages flow like sweet divine.
In colors bright, I scribble fun,
The nonchalant, oh what a run!

Escaping the Educational Grind

Tick-tock goes the classroom clock,
A vessel stuck on dull and stock.
Bored brains drift like trees in fall,
We dream of joy beyond these walls.

Chasing thoughts like butterflies,
As homework piles and knowledge flies.
Math's a maze where I lose my way,
I'd rather play than learn today!

Lunchbox capers and snack-time schemes,
We plot our secrets, share our dreams.
With each recess a daring bid,
To escape on laughter's sweet grid.

So here we are, with banners high,
A world outside, beneath the sky.
No tests or grades, just carefree spins,
In our haven, where fun begins!

Skipping Stones over Curriculum

Stones of knowledge, smooth and round,
We skip them high, where laughter's found.
Curriculum flows like a lazy stream,
We aim for joy, it's our daydream.

Each splash a giggle, twinkling bright,
As boredom takes a daring flight.
Calculators? No chance! We laugh instead,
As rocks leap high, with dreams widespread.

History's lessons become comic strips,
Each date and fact, a twist with quips.
Geography's maps? They swirl and spin,
Adventures await, let the fun begin!

With every toss and every cheer,
We carve out smiles, erase the smear.
Skipping stones, like our carefree minds,
In the water's dance, sweet freedom finds.

Effortless Elegance

Woke up late and missed the bus,
Socks don't match, but who cares, fuss?
Hair's a mess, like a bird's nest,
Strolling in style, feeling my best.

Textbook's blank, but I got the look,
Life's a movie, I'm off the hook.
Teachers stare, but I just grin,
This game of calm, I'm sure to win.

The bell rings loud, but I won't budge,
Gaze at the clouds, give boredom a grudge.
Homework? Nah, that's not my scene,
I float through classes like a chill marine.

Chillin' in the hallway, meme on my phone,
A classroom's chaos feels like a cyclone.
With laughter in tow, I dance on my way,
Effortless elegance, it's just my play.

Trends of the Unstudious

Trends arise, like pizza on Fridays,
Faded jeans and bright hoodies, my personal yay.
Skipping class for the latest craze,
Fashion so loud, it leaves them amazed.

Pop quizzes? Oh, those are so passé,
I'd rather binge watch my favorite play.
Fortnite dances make my heart race,
Winning a match beats any schoolplace.

Scribbled notes contain doodles galore,
Turning the mundane into a chore.
Can't remember who's who, or what's due,
In this style game, I'm the top view.

Skipping school to catch a cool show,
Living life fast, never moving slow.
So if you see me, don't be surprised,
The trends of the unstudious have me mesmerized.

When Apathy Wears Sunglasses

With shades on bright and a yawn so wide,
I shuffle to class, take it in stride.
Apathy's my motto, written in bold,
The golden rule? Be free and uncontrolled.

Teachers drone on, but the sun's to my side,
Daydreaming now, my thoughts take a ride.
What's the lesson? I've long since forgotten,
But my sunglasses? Those are never rotten.

Strolling through halls, I'm chic and aloof,
Chatting 'bout memes, no need for proof.
Grades? Just numbers, they don't mean a thing,
I'll ace this life, let the laughter ring.

In a world of serious, I'll shine bright,
Apathy's a vibe, oh what a delight.
With shades on my face, I swagger and sway,
Fun's the only lesson I'll take away.

The Silent Protest of Youth

Wandering halls, an invisible stance,
Textbooks close, we're not here for romance.
With every skipped class, we make our case,
Turning boredom into a wild embrace.

Pens are down, and doodles begin,
In this classroom riot, let the fun win.
When teachers fret, we're just out for glee,
For knowledge is overrated, you see?

Echoes of laughter, a secret French club,
Raising eyebrows, with a cheeky rub.
A protest of silence, we make our choice,
In the realm of youth, we've found our voice.

Skipping a test, it's a form of art,
Life's our canvas, we play our part.
So here's to the youth, with mischief untamed,
In the game of school, we're proudly unframed.

Witty Words of the Wanderers

In halls where laughter flows like streams,
We share our wild and crafty dreams.
With a wink and nod, we plot away,
Adventures whisper, 'Let's skip today.'

Our backpacks stuffed with snacks and jokes,
We dodge the math, those mean old blokes.
History's tales, we twist and spin,
Each period skipped, a cheeky win!

From lunchroom shenanigans, we rise,
To master tricks, oh what a prize!
With giggles echoing, we roam free,
Learning's a game, a grand jubilee!

So come along, you merry crew,
In the land of fun, there's much to do.
We juggle books and laughter wide,
In this wacky world, we take the ride.

Chilling in the Classroom

In this place where time moves slow,
Chalk dust dances, say hello!
With paper airplanes soaring high,
"Pass the note!" we slyly pry.

The teacher stares, we just can't care,
As worlds unfold in our cool lair.
With every seat a throne to grace,
We plot and scheme, our secret space.

Math's a maze, but jokes we keep,
A treasure trove, not made for sleep.
So while the clock ticks, we persist,
Our laughter rings, an iron fist!

In layers of fun, we pile high,
No work today—just you and I.
Chilling out, we make it clear,
In this class, it's joy we steer!

The Iceberg's Edge of Learning

At the edge where facts float slow,
We warm the ice with a witty glow.
Although some think it's doom and gloom,
We find the fun in every room.

With beakers bubbling, science sizzles,
We mix concoctions, causing giggles.
Geometry? Just shapes we chase,
Daring angles—what a race!

In history's depths we dive so deep,
Sailing ships that never sleep.
The past's just tales, a wild quest,
With friends beside, we're truly blessed.

Plunge into knowledge, break the mold,
In this chilled land, the bold unfold.
We'll learn with flair, never a bore,
At the iceberg's edge, we always soar!

Frosty Tongue and Lively Minds

With frosty breath, we gather round,
Ideas dance, all merry and sound.
Each playful word, a snowball thrown,
In this chill place, we've brightly grown.

Math might freeze our focus tight,
But jokes keep spirits soaring bright.
In science, we concoct our schemes,
Pouring laughter in beaker dreams.

Literature's depths, we bungee dive,
With frosty tongues, we come alive.
History reboots as we unfold,
With humor, each story's retold.

So, gather 'round, you merry band,
With chilling tales that we've planned.
Lively minds in a frosty spree,
In learning's game, we're wild and free!

9 789916 942246